A Gathering of Saints

Some Christian Saints
who were
imprisoned, exiled,
refugees, and penitents.

Edited by Fr Andrew Smith
2019

A Gathering of Saints.
Edited by Rev. Fr Andrew Smith.

First published in 2019.
ISBN: 978-0-244-48548-1

Table of Contents

Foreword

In 2018, I began visiting the Brisbane
Immigration Transit Accommodation
(BITA), where migrant detainees from a
variety of backgrounds resided while they
awaited deliberation from the federal
government. I hoped to teach those who
wanted to be taught, to give comfort and
uplift to those who were downcast, and to
give pastoral care to those who wished it.

One of the things that occurred to me is that
Christianity has a long history of
persecution – from the first century in the
Roman Empire, through to the twentieth
century under Communism, and beyond to
the present day, when in 2019 we find
Christians being the most persecuted group
in the world.

This long history has given us many
brilliant saints – some who were
imprisoned, some exiled from their
homeland, some who were made refugees,

while some turned from a previous life and became examples for us to follow. We have many martyrs and confessors of faith in Jesus Christ. To my joy, some of these saints are collated in this book – and, God willing, others will be collated into future books.

I pray that these will serve, not only by their prayers for us (*James 5:16*), but also by the radiant example that they give to us – that we should follow them, as they follow Christ (*1 Corinthians 11:1*).

In the Risen Christ,
Fr Andrew Smith.

Acknowledgements
from the Editor

A number of people have helped to make this book possible.

Thank you to my wife, whose support for me has been unending and immeasurable.

Thank you to the detainees and staff of Brisbane Immigration Transit Accommodation who attended my talks – whether for a short time or long. Your faith in adversity was and continues to be an inspiration to me.

Thank you to the parishioners of Holy Annunciation Orthodox Church, Brisbane, who were asked to donate towards a book such as this one, and who did so in staggering numbers.

Thank you also to those faithful Orthodox Christians who set aside their time and effort to compile and rewrite the lives of these saints in accessible language – young adults in Southeast Queensland, and people from around the world on Reddit's 'r/OrthodoxChristianity'.

And lastly, thank you to *you*, dear reader. This book is for you. Please keep them and us in your prayers, as we pray for you.

A Prayer for Refugees

O Lord Jesus Christ, our Hope and Salvation, have mercy on those that are driven from their homelands and seek refuge elsewhere. Guide their steps as You did Your holy family who fled the murderous rage of Herod, and keep them from every danger, evil and disaster as they flee from war, unrest, persecution and cruel injustice. You Who declared that the foxes had dens but You had no place to lay Your head, grant rest and succor to those who are weary, wounded and unprotected.

And to those cities and lands to which they travel, grant peace, wisdom and compassion to receive those who come in great numbers and in great distress. Bless and multiply what they can provide, as You multiplied the loaves and the fishes to feed multitudes, blessing those who give as well as those who receive. Enlarge them in bounty and spirit that they may be havens of rest and relief to those in need, that Your hospitality may overcome the madness of evil men and chaos of natural disasters.

Forgive every transgression of those who are forced to leave their homes and have mercy also on those who receive them and offer them shelter, for You are good and the lover of mankind.

To You our gracious Lord and God, we ascribe glory, together with Your Father Who is from everlasting and the all-holy, good and life-giving Holy Spirit, now and ever and unto ages of ages. Amen.

Prophet Daniel and the Three Holy Youths

Imprisoned for refusing idolatry

Nebuchadnezzar was the King of a city called Babylon. 597 years before the birth of Jesus Christ, Nebuchadnezzar captured the city of Jerusalem. After he captured the city, he took many royal people from there back to Babylon. He wanted the "best" people so he could train them to serve in his palace. Of these royal people, there was an eight year old boy named Daniel and his three friends Ananias, Azariah and Mishael. They were handsome youths, and were picked to learn the language of the Nebuchadnezzar's kingdom so they would be able to serve in the King's service.

Their names meant:
- 'Daniel': The Lord is my judge
- 'Ananias': The Lord is kind
- 'Azarias': God is my help
- 'Misael': Who is like God

The King then ordered them to be given new names:

- Daniel became 'Belteshazzar' which means Keeper of Bel's treasures ('Bel' was a pagan idol);
- Ananias became 'Shadrach', meaning "the inspiration of the sun";
- Azarias became 'Abednego', meaning "the slave of the sun"; and,
- Misael became 'Meshach', meaning "of the goddess Shach" (Shach was also a pagan idol).

The original names of the young men showed the qualities of God, the true God. They were given new names to change their identities and show them as followers of pagan idols, trying to force them to forget their original belief in the true God because the King and the people of his land were pagans who worshipped idols instead.

But Daniel and the three youths kept the law of the Lord, even though they lived with the pagan people. They would not even eat the food of the King's table because it was animals that had been killed to worship idols. They would eat vegetables and water and continued to pray to the one true God instead. The King's chief who was in charge of looking after the youth said to Daniel that he was afraid that they would get thin and sick from not eating the meat and the chief would be in trouble with the King. So Daniel and the three youths asked to be put under the test for ten days of fasting. At the end of the ten days, they appeared healthier and better looking than all the other children in the King's court – because their goal was to please God. God rewarded them and gave them wisdom and knowledge so that they were smarter than all the educated men in the Kingdom. Daniel was also given by God the gift of interpreting dreams and visions.

Three years later the King had a dream which made him afraid and so he asked all the wise men of the kingdom to tell him what it meant. The wise men asked the

King what the dream was, but the King said he had forgotten the dream and would kill them all if they did not tell him what it meant. They said it was impossible to interpret a dream which they had not been told of, so the King got angry and made an announcement to kill all the wise men in the kingdom, including Daniel and his three friends.

When the captain of the King's guards, Arioch, came to kill Daniel and his three friends, Daniel asked what they were being killed for, and Arioch explained. So Daniel went to the king and asked him to give him time to find out what the King's dream meant. Daniel went home to his three friends and told them what had happened. Together they prayed to God, asking for His mercy and to reveal the meaning of the dream to them. They prayed saying:

> *"Blessed be the name of God forever and ever,*
> *For wisdom and might are His.*
> *And He changes the times and the seasons;*

*He removes kings and raises up
    kings;*
He gives wisdom to the wise
*And knowledge to those who have
    understanding.*
He reveals deep and secret things;
He knows what is in the darkness,
And light dwells with Him.
I thank You and praise You,
O God of my fathers;
*You have given me wisdom and
    might,*
*And have now made known to me
    what we asked of You,*
*For You have made known to us the
    king's demand."*

God revealed the meaning of the dream to Daniel and so he went to the Arioch, saying, "Do not kill the wise men of Babylon, and I will tell the interpretation to the king". So the captain took Daniel to the King, and he said to the King, "The wise men cannot tell you the meaning of your secret dream. But there is a God in heaven who reveals secrets and He has revealed it to me – not because I have more wisdom, but so that you may know the thoughts of your heart." (*Daniel 2:30*) Daniel then told the King his dream and what it meant. So the king made Daniel the chief and ruler over all of Babylon. Daniel asked that his three friends come with him, and the King also gave the three friends important positions over the affairs of Babylon.

A few years later, King Nebuchadnezzar built a large, golden idol and commanded everyone in his kingdom to fall down and worship the golden idol at the sound of trumpets. Some wise men were jealous of the high positions that the King had given Daniel's three friends Ananias, Azariah and Mishael, so they told the King that the three friends would not worship the idol and, therefore, should be punished. The King was very angry that the three friends would not worship the idol so he ordered a very big oven to be filled with fire 7 times hotter than normal. It was so hot that the guards who threw the three friends into the fire died from the fire's heat. But, the three friends prayed to God, and he sent His Angel to protect them. The Angel surrounded the youths in a cool, wet breeze as they stood in the middle of the fire, so they were not burnt.

The king saw this and said: "I see four men, walking in the midst of the fire, and they are not hurt, and the form of the forth is like the Son of God" (*Daniel 3:24,25*). He called to the three friends and asked them to come out of the fire and permitted the worship of the one true God.

The Mother of God, and, Saint Joseph: The Flight into Egypt

Voluntary exile for fear of murder

After the three wise men had gone home, God sent down an Angel to warn Saint Joseph that the evil King Herod was going to send his soldiers to kill the infant Jesus. With worry in his heart and fear for his family, Joseph quickly gathered together what they could carry, to escape into the darkness of the night.

The Mother of God holding her precious boy close to her heart, wrapped Him in warm blankets and soothed Him to sleep as they packed up and made ready for the trip ahead. With just a few of their things, Saint Joseph led the donkey with the Child and His mother sitting on top, into the cold of the night with nothing to protect them other than God's help.

As they travelled the long-used dusty road to Egypt, where other Jews had also fled before, the family felt the danger behind them. They worried that the soldiers would reach them before they could cross into the borders of Egypt. Travelling as quickly as one could with a child, they suffered many difficulties along the way. The cold and heat of each day and sleeping out on the hard ground made their bodies tired and their spirits low. The constant pressure to find food and safety as well as looking out for danger made them all feel worn out. But they put up with this heavy load of responsibility without complaint and accepted it, trusting in God's plan.

Although God is not afraid of soldiers or any other power, He was now living on Earth as a human, feeling all the fear, cold, hunger and sadness that we face. He felt human weakness, with no miracles to make this journey easy, until He was ready to show Himself to the world. He hid Himself in His human form, running from danger as a human, to suffer all that we suffer on Earth, just to show us that He as God himself has in truth become man. Even now as a Child on the run, He suffered the dangers of a refugee.

Driven from His home with His Blessed Mother, the family made their way slowly to the safe borders of a strange country. At the time, this country was one that practiced all sorts of cults and false beliefs of the evil one, and worshipping Pharaoh as if he was a deity. Christ, God Himself, came to seek shelter in a pagan country. With this journey an ancient prediction had taken place: Out of Egypt I have called my Son (*Hosea 11:1*). This broadcasts that He has come into the world to end godless or pagan worship, and to bring understanding of the Truth to His people!

After a few years, an Angel of God was sent down again to Joseph to tell him that it was safe to go home. Joseph listened to the order given him, and he took his family back along the long road to Palestine. On their return from Egypt, they headed for

Galilee and settled in a little town called
Nazareth. Here in this town they stayed
and were safely far enough from Jerusalem,
where Herod's cruel son Archelaus was
now in power. Jesus lived here and grew in
His wisdom until He was ready to show
himself to the world.

Saint John the Baptist

Imprisoned for speaking truth to power

Some months before the birth of Jesus Christ, an angel told Zacharias and Elizabeth that they will finally have a baby, and that they should name him John. The angel said John "will be great in the sight of the Lord" (*Luke 1:15*) because he will prepare the hearts of the people, to be ready for the Lord. Zacharias and Elizabeth were "righteous before God" (*Luke 1:6*), and were quite old when the angel made this announcement.

John was "filled with the Holy Spirit, even from his mother's womb" (*Luke 1:15*). When Elizabeth was pregnant, the angel Gabriel announced to her cousin, Mary, that Mary will become the mother of Jesus. Mary, now pregnant also, came to visit Elizabeth. When Elizabeth heard the greeting of Mary, John the baby leaped in

Elizabeth's womb with joy because he recognized Jesus as the Son of God.

After Jesus, the Son of God, was born in Bethlehem, wise men from the East told King Herod that a baby, born King of the Jews, had been born in Bethlehem. Herod sent soldiers to Bethlehem to kill all children younger than two years old. Not satisfied with this killing of the innocent children, Herod knew about the unusual birth of John to very elderly parents, so he sent soldiers to kill him also. The Righteous Elizabeth ran away with John into the wilderness, praying to God for their safety. Immediately, the hill opened up and made a space for them to hide in. When the soldiers could not find Elizabeth and John, they went to the temple where the Righteous Zachariah was serving as priest. He refused to tell Herod where Elizabeth had fled to, so the soldiers killed him in the temple. Forty days later, Elizabeth died in the wilderness hiding place. The Lord was with the young child John.

When John had grown up, he lived in the desert, wearing camel skins, with a leather belt around his waist. He ate locusts and wild honey, living like an angel of the desert. As a prophet, he gave knowledge of salvation to the Lord's people. He also baptized many as they confessed their sins. Saint John the Baptist baptised many people in the Jordan River, saying, "Repent, for the kingdom of heaven is at hand!" (*Matthew 3:2*). Saint John said that while he baptises with water, Jesus will "baptise you with the Holy Spirit and fire", that Jesus is "mightier than I, whose sandals I am not worthy to carry" (*Matthew 3:11*).

Saint John the Baptist is also called the Forerunner: the person who came before Jesus to teach that Jesus is the Saviour. Hundreds of years before Jesus was born, the Prophets said,

> *"Behold, I send My messenger before Your face, Who will prepare Your way before You."*
> *"The voice of one crying in the wilderness: 'Prepare the way of the Lord; Make His paths straight.'" (Mark 1:2-3)*

Saint John was this messenger who prepared the way for Jesus Christ. He was the voice crying out in the desert to make straight the paths, like royal messengers who paved and repaired roads before the king visits an area.

Jesus said that John "was the burning and shining lamp, and you were willing for a time to rejoice in his light" (*John 5:35*). Even though John recognized that Jesus was greater, nonetheless Jesus asked John to baptize him. The Orthodox Church celebrates this every year in January at a feast called 'Theophany' ('the revealing of God'), because while Jesus prayed after His baptism, the heaven was opened, and the Holy Spirit descended in the form of a dove and landed on Him, and a voice came from heaven which said, "You are My beloved Son; in You I am well pleased." (*Luke 3:21-22*)

When Saint John criticized Herod the tetrarch for marrying his living brother's wife, Herodias, it made Herodias very angry. She convinced Herod to imprison him; and later, Herod had John the Baptist killed.

Saint George

*Imprisoned and brutally killed
for refusing idolatry*

Saint George was a talented military officer
who amazed the world by his military
exploits in the 3rd century. He died before
he was even thirty years old. He is known
as Victory Bearer, not only for his military
success, but for courageously enduring
fierce torments and martyrdom. His
unrelenting faith and courage converted
many to believe in Christ during his trials,
and he continues to aid those who
supplicate him to this day.

Saint George entered the service of the
Roman army. He was handsome, brave and
valiant in battle, and he came to the notice
of the emperor Diocletian (284-305) and
joined the imperial guard.

What is Truth?" one of the dignitaries
asked, echoing the question of Pontius

Pilate. The saint replied, "Christ Himself, Whom you persecuted, is Truth."

Stunned by the bold speech of the valiant warrior, the emperor, who had loved and promoted George, attempted to persuade him not to throw away his youth and glory and honours, but rather to offer sacrifice to the gods as was the Roman custom. The confessor replied, "Nothing in this inconstant life can weaken my resolve to serve God."

The enraged officers sent Saint George out of the assembly hall with spears and led him off to prison. But the deadly steel became soft and it bent when the spears touched the saint's body, and it caused him no harm.

The exploits and miracles of the Saint George had already converted many to Christianity, therefore Diocletian made a new attempt to persuade the saint to offer sacrifice to idols. They set up a court at the pagan temple of Apollo. During the night the holy martyr prayed fervently, and as he slept, he saw the Lord, Who raised him up and embraced him. The Saviour placed a crown on Saint George's head and said, "Fear not, but have courage, and you will soon come to Me and receive what has been prepared for you."

The next day at the interrogation, Saint George said to the emperor, "You will grow tired of tormenting me sooner than I will tire of being tormented by you." Then Diocletian gave orders to subject Saint George to some very intense tortures. They tied the him to a wheel, beneath which were boards pierced with sharp pieces of iron. As the wheel turned, the sharp edges slashed the saint's naked body. At first the sufferer loudly cried out to the Lord, but soon he did not utter even a single groan. Diocletian thought that the Saint was already dead, and he gave orders to remove the battered body, and then went to a pagan temple to offer thanks. At this very moment it got dark, thunder boomed, and a voice was heard: "Fear not, George, for I am with you." Then a wondrous light shone, and at the wheel an angel of the Lord appeared in the form of a radiant youth. He placed his hand upon the martyr, saying to him, "Rejoice!" Saint George stood up healed. When the soldiers led him to the pagan temple where the emperor was, the emperor could not believe his own eyes and he thought that he saw before him a ghost. In confusion and in terror the pagans looked Saint George over carefully, and they became convinced that a miracle had occurred. Many then came to believe in the Life-Creating God of the Christians.

The emperor became even more furious, so he gave him over to more fearsome torments. After throwing him into a deep pit, they covered it over with lime. Three days later they dug him out, but found him cheerful and unharmed. They forced the saint to wear iron sandals with red-hot nails, and then drove him back to the prison with whips. In the morning, when they led him back to the interrogation, cheerful and with healed feet, the emperor asked if he liked his shoes. The saint said that the sandals had been just his size. Then they beat him with ox thongs until pieces of his flesh came off and his blood soaked the ground, but the brave sufferer, strengthened by the power of God, remained unyielding.

Then the emperor asked what sort of power was helping him, Saint George said, "Do not imagine that it is any human learning which keeps me from being harmed by these torments. I am saved only by calling upon Christ and His Power. Whoever believes in Him has no regard for tortures and is able to do the things that Christ did" (John 14:12). Diocletian asked what sort of things Christ had done. The Martyr replied, "He gave sight to the blind, cleansed the lepers, healed the lame, gave hearing to the deaf, cast out demons, and raised the dead."

The emperor offered to make Saint George second only to himself. The holy martyr with a feigned willingness answered, "Caesar, you should have shown me this mercy from the very beginning, instead of torturing me. Let us go now to the temple and see the gods you worship." Diocletian believed that the martyr was accepting his offer, and he followed him to the pagan temple with his retinue and all the people. Everyone was certain that Saint George would offer sacrifice to the gods. The saint went up to the idol, made the Sign of the Cross and addressed it as if it were alive: "Are you the one who wants to receive from me sacrifice befitting God?" The demon inhabiting the idol cried out, "I am not a god and none of those like me is a god, either. The only God is He Whom you preach. We are fallen angels, and we deceive people because we are jealous." Saint George cried out boldly, "How dare you remain here, when I, the servant of the true God, have entered?" Then noises and wailing were heard from the idols, and they fell to the ground and were shattered.

Diocletian immediately pronounced the death sentence on the Great Martyr. Saint George gave thanks to God and prayed that he would also end his life in a worthy manner. At the place of execution the saint prayed that the Lord would forgive the torturers who acted in ignorance, and that He would lead them to the knowledge of Truth. Calmly and bravely, the holy Great Martyr George bent his neck beneath the sword, receiving the crown of martyrdom in 303AD.

Within ten years, Saint Constantine, as Emperor, would issue the Edict of Milan, granting religious freedom to Christians.

Saint Luke of Simferopol

Repeatedly imprisoned for faith in Christ

Born in 1877, the future saint was raised in a Christian family, with his first true understanding of Christianity coming from a copy of the New Testament, which was given to him by his high school principal.

He studied art, before graduating as a doctor and then as an eye surgeon. He married Anna, a nurse, and they had four children. They moved frequently to regional health care facilities, following his career, and he would never request funds from his patients or turn anyone away because of ethnicity or beliefs. In 1917, he rose to be head surgeon and professor at Tashkent hospital. However, when the atheistic Communists took over government, he was under continuous threat, but he was valued for his exceptional surgical ability.

After his wife died, he never remarried. He was ordained a priest in 1921, and served in addition to his work as a doctor. Soon after, he was arrested, put on trial and, despite lacking any proof, sentenced him to 16 years imprisonment. Just before he was put in prison, he was made a bishop, and while he was in prison, he would always be placed at a medical facility. He was released in 1926, after just three years, but was arrested again in 1930 and sentenced to exile for three years.

After his release, he was very prominent in the medical community, including publishing the defining textbook for a medical specialty (still used today) – for which he was awarded a doctorate in 1936. He continued service as a bishop, supporting parishes and priests, and raising hunger strikes against injustices to fellow Christians. As his fame grew, the Communist authorities would transfer him. In 1937 he was again arrested, and spent over two years in torture, interrogation and humiliation. He endured all of these, trusting in the Lord. He not only refuted false accusations against him, but he protested – refusing to eat and sending complaints to authorities against illegal actions he saw. His fellow prisoners saw his character – never charging for his medical care, and sharing the pain of his patients and fellow inmates.

In 1940, he was sentenced to five years of exile, to be served in Krasnoyarsk. When Russia entered World War II, he offered his services as a doctor, and in 1941 was made consultant to the hospitals there. Through his work as the local archbishop, he was even able to open a church where he could serve in 1943. He was transferred to Tambov in 1944.

In 1946, St Luke was transferred to Crimea, combining service as a bishop with his medical work, until the government prohibited him from practicing medicine and he was then able to devote himself to Church service – which, with Russia being under the Communists, demanded great courage and faith. He preached about the need for the people to live their faith, and to not accept any false compromises.

St Luke's persecution by the authorities had the effect of increasing his popularity. Despite government slander, he was known to be loving and unselfish. He performed many healing miracles, and was known as an exceptional guide in the spiritual life.

St Luke died on June 11, 1961. The people ignored the atheistic government's protests and ensured a full funeral service, with procession to the gravesite, took place, with all reverence. He was officially recognised as a saint in 1996. During this process of recognition, it was discovered that his heart was fully intact, while his bones gave a sweet smell – both of which testified to the great love he bore for Christ and his neighbour.

Saint Dismas the Wise Thief

Repentant at the end

St Dismas was a thief, and for his crimes he was punished. He was crucified alongside Jesus, as was another thief.

In the Gospels, the thieves are seen taunting Jesus (*Matthew 27:44, Mark 15:32*), but Dismas must have had a change of heart. The other thief continues to mock Him, but Dismas rebukes him – noting that while they were receiving the punishment for what they had done, Jesus was being punished for what He had *not* done. He asks Jesus to remember him when Jesus comes into His Kingdom. Jesus answers that Dismas will be with Him in paradise that day (*Luke 23:39-43*).

St Dismas gives us an example of someone who had done wrong things, who was still able to turn their life to Christ – and know that he was accepted and forgiven by God.

The name of 'Dismas' wasn't given to us in the Bible. Instead, we learn his name from a fourth-century writing.

In the Eastern Orthodox services for Good Friday, remembering the Crucifixion of Christ, we sing a hymn about St Dismas. In that hymn, we note that Jesus made St Dismas – called the 'Wise Thief' – worthy of heaven in a single moment, and we ask that we be enlightened like he was. We also remember him in our prayers before Communion – that we will confess Christ like St Dismas did, with humility.

We commemorate him each year on March 25 or April 7.

Saint Mary of Egypt

Repentant from a sin-loving life

Mary was an Egyptian who left her parents at the age of 12 to pursue a life of sin and lust, which lasted for 17 years. She was not forced into this life by a need for money, but wanted it out of passionate desire. One day, she wanted to enter the Church of the Resurrection in Jerusalem, but was stopped from entering by a power she could not see, while other Christians could enter easily. She realised it was her sinful way of life that was stopping her from entering this holy place. She admitted her sinfulness before God, and prayed with deep feeling and pain to the icon of the Mother of God that she be let into the Church to honour the cross, saying, 'if I am allowed to honour His Cross, I promise I will turn away from my life of pleasure, and follow the path of salvation that you show me.'

She felt herself suddenly freed from the power stopping her, and could then enter the church. She bowed to the cross, and then said to the icon of the Mother of God that she was ready to follow the path showed to her. A voice replied to her from the heavens: 'if you cross the Jordan River, if you will find rest.' She then left the church and bought three loaves of bread with money that a Christian traveler gave her. After washing in the river, she then received Communion at the Church of St John the Baptist, ate half her bread, and fell asleep on the riverbank. The next morning, she crossed the river and lived in the desert for forty-seven years without seeing another person or animal during this time.

Her clothes became rags, and she burned with heat by day and shook with cold by night. For the first seventeen years she ate only herbs and wild roots. But, harder than these physical challenges was her struggle with memories of her past life of sin and lust. But she prayed through this, asking the Mother of God to help her. By the protection of God who loves us all, she uprooted this sin from her heart with patience and hard work, and turned it into divine love that helped her endure the desert with joy.

After all these years, a holy elder called Zosimas, travelled into the desert for Great Lent. At this time, from a distance, he saw a body blackened by the sun with shoulder length hair as white as snow. He ran after that person, not knowing her to be a woman, seeking a blessing and healing words. When he came closer, Mary called him by name, even though she had never met him before, and she said that she needed his cloak to cover her nakedness.

At the urging of Zosimas, with tears Mary told the story of her life and conversion to Christ. After she told her story, she begged him to come the following year with Holy Communion. The following year Zosimas arrived at the riverbank and saw Mary waiting for him. She made the sign of the cross, and crossed the river by walking on the water. After receiving Holy Communion, while crying tears of joy she said a prayer of thanksgiving to God and asked Zosimas to return next year in the place they had first met.

When the year was past, Zosimas was travelling to the agreed spot and found the Saints' body with her arms crossed and her face turned toward the East. He cried, and saw that she had written her name in the dirt, asked that he bury her there and say a prayer for her. She had also written that her death followed receiving Holy Communion on April 1st, the night our Lord and Saviour Jesus Christ was crucified that year.

Zosimas's grief was eased to learn her name, and amazed when he realised she had, in several hours, travelled a distance of 20 days' march. After vainly trying to dig a burial pit for her with a stick, a lion approached and licked the Saints feet. Zosimas requested the lion to dig a hole with its claws, in which he placed the Saint's body.

When Zosimas returned to his monastery, he told all of the mercy and love that God provided for those who turn away from sin and look for him with all their hearts. From the sinner she had been, Mary has provided hope to many souls hurting and weighed down by sin. This is why, in the Orthodox Church, she is remembered on the last Sunday of Great Lent, to encourage those who have neglected their salvation, proclaiming that repentance can always bring them back to God – even when it seems like it's too little or too late.

Saint Moses the Black

Repentant from a violent life

Moses the Ethiopian was a slave who stole from his master. His behaviour was so bad that his master decided that he would be better off without him and sent him away. Free from slavery, Moses continued his thievery and became the leader of a gang of criminals who stopped at nothing to steal, including murder.

One day however, Moses had a serious accident which humbled him greatly. Seeing his life flash before his eyes, he realised his error and the love of Christ touched his heart. From that moment on, Moses decided to turn away from his past life, to turn away from his sinful ways and to turn towards Christ in repentance. After having been baptised, he went into the desert to a place far away called Scetis, which was home to many hermits and monastics. With little water and nobody to speak with, his body became weathered and dry as he worked hard in the sun.

One day, four robbers attacked him while Moses was resting in his cell. With his mighty strength, Moses overpowered the men, tied them up and carried them to church saying: 'I am not permitted to do harm to anyone. What do you, our Lord God, want of these men?' When the four robbers realised who Moses was, the infamous leader of the criminal gang, they were amazed. They said to each other that, if such a man can come into God's service, then we too can be saved! And so, they became monks as well.

Even though Moses repented, prayed deeply and fasted, he was continuously attacked by his passions, especially the demon of fornication. One day, when he was on the edge of despair, he decided to visit the priest of Scetis, the great Elder Isidore. The Elder told him that he shouldn't be surprised at having to face such violent battles. He explained that this was like a dog in a butcher's shop, who is used to chewing on bones, and cannot give up the habit until there are no more bones to chew on – in the same way, it is not enough for the sinner to stop committing the sin, but also, the bad habit must be driven away by the good habit of virtue, along with denial of the flesh over many years.

Upon hearing this, Moses was given strength and the demon began to despair. Without the means of feeding the impure desires in Moses' heart, the demon gave up the struggle. On returning to his cell, Moses gave himself over to extremely strict fasting. He only ate a little bread, gave himself to hard labour, and read fifty groups of prayers each day. Yet even though he tried to crucify his flesh, the passions still attacked him, especially in his dreams.

Moses returned to the cell of the great Elder Isidore for advice. The Elder told him that if he wanted purity of mind, he could have this through vigils and more hard labour. So, Moses went back and added fasts and all-night vigils every night, standing in the middle of his cell and praying without closing his eyes. When thoughts continued to attack him, he perfected the building of a new man within himself by the passionate love for his fellow brothers. At night, he went to the cells of old hermits who no longer had the strength to carry water, and he took their jars to collect water for them a few miles away.

The demon, furious at seeing his control weakened, attacked Moses one night while he was leaning over the well and cracked him on the back of the head with a club. The next day, one of the brothers who had gone to collect water found him lying there, half dead. The brother hurried back to tell the Elder and bring help.

Taken back to the Church, Moses took a year to recover his strength. Elder Isidore urged Moses to stop provoking the demons to battle, as there is a limit in all things, but Christ's brave soldier replied: 'I cannot stop while the images suggested by the demons continue to trouble me.' The Elder then told him that he would from this moment on be freed from dreams, and that this temptation had been allowed by God so that he would not boast of overcoming these passions in his own strength. Moses returned to his cell; and, after two months, went back to Elder Isidore to tell him that he was experiencing no more trouble.

As well as this incredible gift, God also gave Moses power over the demons, and changed his violent nature into an unparalleled charity and gentleness. One day, a brother committed a serious sin at Scetis and the fathers were gathering around to judge him. They invited Abba Moses to join them, but he refused. While the fathers were waiting for Moses to join, a priest was sent to go find him. Seeing this, Moses got up, took up a leaking basket, filled it with sand and began to head towards the assembly. The priest who was sent for him approached and asked: 'What is going on, Father?' Moses answered: 'My sins run down behind me and I do not see them, and I have come today to judge someone else's fault!' When the fathers heard this, they repented, said nothing to the brother at fault and forgave him.

One day a brother had gone to Scetis to visit the Elder there. He wanted to see the famous Elder Arsenius, but the elder would not see him. The brother then went to see Abba Moses, who received him with joy and kindness. Bothered by this difference in attitude, the brother asked God to show him how, whilst both serving God, one elder could receive the brothers company and the other deny him.

God heard his prayer and answered him through a dream. He was shown two great barges on a river, and saw Elder Arsenius and the Spirit of God floating in one in great peace; and, in the other, Abba Moses and the angels of God, who were feeding him honey cakes.

Having grown close to God, Abba Moses was made a priest, by the example of his virtues, he converted seventy of his former robber-band, who became his disciples. He taught them to free themselves from the passions by spiritual exercise, and to live in their cells as though in the grave, dead to all men. Moses said: 'To die to your neighbour means…to bear your own faults, we shall not see those of our own neighbour. It is useless for a man who has a dead person in his house to leave him there and to go weep over his neighbour's dead.' When he was asked the reason of all the hard labour, spiritual exercise and fasting, he replied: 'They make the soul humble…for if the soul gives itself all this hardship, God will have mercy on it.'

Abba Moses was seventy-five years old when news came that barbarians were about to attack Scetis. All the monks prepared to flee except for Abba Moses. Confused, the brothers asked why he was remaining there with such peace, he replied: 'I have been waiting for this day for many years, that the word of the Lord Christ may be fulfilled which says: All who take to the sword will perish by the sword (*Matthew 26:52*). Edified by his reply, the brothers said to him: "we will not leave either, but we will die with you.' Abba Moses said to them: 'That is nothing to do with me, let everyone decide for himself whether he stays or not, and do as the Lord reveals to him.'

The barbarians ripped through the famous monastic centre of Scetis, killing without mercy all whom they found there. When they reached the cell of Abba Moses and his seven disciples, one of the monks was able to hide behind a heap of rope and, when the holy fathers were massacred, he saw crowns descend from heaven and lie on their bodies.

Saint Clement of Rome

Exiled for faith in Christ

St Clement of Rome was born in Rome into a wealthy family. He was raised by strangers after being separated from his parents. Money did not make him happy, and he began to wonder about the meaning of life

St Clement heard about the good news of Jesus Christ and went to visit the apostles, the students of Christ and listen to them preach about God. He met an Apostle, named Barnabas. His words were powerful and Clement felt truth when he heard them.

Clement arrived in Palestine and was baptized by the Apostle Peter. Then, he became a dedicated disciple, and they suffered together through lots of pain and suffering. Before Saint Peter died, he made Saint Clement the Bishop of Rome. In the year 92 to 101, St Clement was the head of the church in Rome.

St Clement lived an honourable life to God, always doing charitable works and prayerful activities, he converted lots of people to Christ. On a single Easter day, he baptized 424 people. People of all levels and from all backgrounds were baptized such as slaves, officials and members of the royal family.

The pagans, who were not Christians, did not like his success, so they told the Emperor Trajan that Saint Clement had insulted the pagan Gods. The emperor banished Saint Clement from the main city and sent him to Crimea as an exile, to work in a stone quarry. Many of his followers went with him to support him and be with him.

When he arrived at the place he was sent to, he found many other Christians there, who were also forced to do hard labour with not much water around. He prayed to God with them, and God appeared in the form of a small lamb, to lead them where the water was in the ground. Water came flowing out like a river. The miracle made lots of people want to listen to Saint Clement, after they heard him talk about God and the Gospel, hundreds of non-believers where converted to Christianity that day, and around 500 were baptized that day. They built a church in the stone quarry, where he celebrated divine services.

The emperor who sent him away go very mad at him for converting people and ordered he be drowned and killed. They threw him into the sea with an anchor tied around his neck in the year 101, and so he was martyred for his faith in Christ.

Saint Clements loyal friends and disciples prayed to God that they could see his body again. The sea drew back about 7 kilometers from the shore line and people could walk out to find a marble cave shaped like a church. There they found his body in perfect condition in an Angelic Form, made by God.

Every year for 7 days the sea would pull back to people could visit his body and pay respects to it. For many years the sea pulled back for people to visit his body. Now, his body is in different Churches for us to pay our respects to.

Saint Clement has left a great spiritual legacy for us, including some of the first writings and letters of the Christian Church.

Saint Maximus the Confessor

Exiled for teaching Christian truth

Saint Maximus the Confessor was an Orthodox Christian monk who was also an academic and scholar. The saint was born in the area of modern day Turkey. He was very well educated and spent time working in the Government before he became a monk.

In the year 640 he started to publicly oppose a teaching that was common at the time, about how the divine and human interacted in Jesus. Even though it was revealed that Jesus is both God and human (and had a divine nature and a human nature), this false teaching taught that He only had one will. Maximus taught that if a nature didn't have a will, then it was not a nature at all – instead, the divine and human will were both aligned in Jesus.

Because the saint disagreed with the false teaching, he was taken to the capital of the Eastern Roman Empire at the time, Constantinople, and was pressured to agree with the teaching that Jesus had one will. The saint refused to accept this wrong teaching, and he was then sent against his will to another country.

After some time the government changed, and Maximus was allowed to come back. The saint continued to work to persuade people to understand and accept the correct way of thinking. The saint was taken to the rulers for questioning, and then they his tongue and right hand. Both of these were to prevent him from preaching and writing the truth about Jesus.

The saint was sent against his will to another country again and he died shortly after. The saint was later declared innocent and was recognized as a Father of the Church. Many of his writings are still used today.

Saint Paisios the Athonite

Exiled for being the wrong race

> *St Paisios was asked: "Elder, what should we do with the refugees that come to our country? Should we help them?".*
> *He responded: "My child, you know the answer. Didn't the Lord say that every person is Him; that in every person we should see Christ? And what does it say in the Bible? 'I was a foreigner, a stranger and you took care of me' and thus you should be with me in Paradise."*

Elder Paisios was a refugee from Cappadocia, in Asia Minor (which is now part of Turkey). He lived all the drama of being uprooted, and he experienced through his own family and friends the pain, the blood, the fury and the hatred against his countrymen.

This genuine man of God was born to devoted and faithful parents, Prodromos and Eulambia, at Farasa in Cappadocia (modern-day Turkey) on the 25th of July, 1924. A month after he was born, his family and city were forced to abandon their ancestral lands by the government, and were exiled to Greece. Just before they left, the teacher and priest of the village, Saint Arsenios of Cappadocia, baptized the baby, naming the baby after himself.

The boat arrived in Greece in September. They lived in Piraeus, then Corfu, then Konitsa, where he finished primary school. As a child, Arsenios would write down the miracles of the priest who had baptised him, would fast and pray constantly, and would study the lives of the saints.

He had already decided to pursue the monastic life; however, his parents would not give him a blessing until he was old enough to grow a beard. He was obedient in this matter.

He took up carpentry, learning the craft and demonstrating a good working character. When given a job, he was known for thoroughness and cheerfulness, and would share his small income with the poor of the village, and any requests for coffins were completed free of charge.

He was enlisted in the army in 1945, and was made a radio transmitter. He would request to be in the first line of defence, because he didn't want his fellow soldiers with families to be hurt.

In 1949, Arsenios went to Mount Athos, mountain filled with monasteries and monks, to fulfil his lifelong dream to become a monk. He was tonsured a monk in 1954, and lived in a number of monasteries and hermitages on Mount Athos.

He became ill in the late 1980s, before passing away in mid-1994. He was buried at a monastery in Souroti, Thessaloniki, a city in Greece. Thousands have come to his grave to honour him and to pay their respects to this saint who endured so much.

He was known for his prayer for the world, doing good to all – regardless of their race and religion.

Saint Maria Skobtsova

A Refugee from Atheism and Communism

Born in an upper-class family in Latvia in 1891, the future saint was named 'Elizaveta Pilenko'. When she was a teenager, her father died and she embraced atheism. When her mother took the family to St Petersburg in 1906, she became involved in radical intellectual circles, authoring poetry. She married a Bolshevik Communist in 1910, which ended in 1913.

Turning from Communism, she was attracted to Christianity through looking at the sufferings and death of Jesus Christ. She moved south with her daughter, and her devotion increased.

In 1918, after the Russian Revolution, she was elected deputy mayor of her town. When the opposing army took control of the town, she became mayor, but was put on trial for supporting the other side.

Fortunately, the judge was a former teacher and she was acquitted. Soon after, she and that judge fell in love and got married.

With political turmoil continuing, the family fled the country, travelling to Georgia and Yugoslavia before arriving in Paris in 1923. Elizaveta dedicated herself to learning about God and helping the community.

One of her three children died of the flu, and the family was torn apart by divorce. Elizaveta devoted herself to work in the community. Her bishop encouraged her to do this work as a nun, and she was given the name 'Maria'. Her monastic labours were to provide an open door for refugees, the needy, and the lonely. It quickly became a centre of discussion about God and other matters. For St Maria, service and theology were two sides of the same coin.

In World War II, Jews approached the house asking for baptismal certificates so that they wouldn't be killed by the Nazis, which St Maria's chaplain provided. Many Jews came to stay with them, and they helped many escape. Eventually, the house was closed down, and Saint Maria was taken by the Nazi Secret Police, and was sent to a concentration camp in Ravensbrück. She was killed in 1945, taking the place of someone else who had been selected for death.

The Holy Synod of the Church of Constantinople glorified St Maria in 2004 as a martyr for the Christian faith, and she is commemorated each year on July 20. She is remembered for her hospitality and her uncompromising love for the people around her, which she considered to be the foundation of the Christian Gospel.

Saint Jonah of Hankou

A Refugee from Atheism and Communism

Born in Russia in 1886 Jonah was orphaned when he was eight years old. The church deacon took him in and made sure he received an education. He then went on to graduate from the Theological Academy, where he became a monk and, later, a lecturer.

He was later ordained a priest and continued to teach until the Bolsheviks took power. The Bolsheviks were opposed to God and religion.

Saint Jonah was arrested and beaten until he was knocked out. He managed to escape the police and joined a volunteer army as their chaplain. The volunteer army retreated into China where many Russians had fled to avoid being tortured by the Bolsheviks.

The Russian refugees were very poor, many had only the clothes they were wearing. During this time in China, Saint Jonah became a Bishop. He cared for his people and prayed for them often. He became an inspiration to his people in China.

His main concern was the commandment to love one's neighbour. He opened a library, soup kitchen, a medical clinic and a school. He also set up an orphanage that cared for 28 children in its first year.

The saint gave himself fully to everything that he did. After caring for a priest who was ill with fever, he contracted chronic throat pain. Even with his chronic pain, he continued to serve his flock. One day he rinsed his throat with fuel, thinking that it would work to clean his throat, but this led to blood poisoning.

The saint realised that death was near, and he started to prepare himself to be with the Lord. He read the canon for the departure of the soul, and lay down on his bed and said "God's will be done, now I shall die". Within minutes he had passed from this life into the other world which knows 'neither sickness, nor sighs, nor sorrow but life everlasting in the joy of the Lord'.

On the night of his funeral, all of the people mourned. Soon after, the saint appeared to a paralysed ten year old boy, and healed him.

Afterword

Thank you for reading this book. I hope that it has brought comfort and hope, knowing that many Christians have experienced problems and difficulties, and have been glorified by God as His holy people.

I am grateful to be the priest at two parishes:

- *Holy Annunciation Orthodox Church* is Brisbane's English-language Orthodox parish.
  Find out more at:
  www.HolyAnnunciation.net

- *St John the Baptist Orthodox Mission* is the Orthodox church in Toowoomba. Find out more at:
  www.OrthodoxToowoomba.com

If you find yourself in either place, please feel free to contact me. I would be delighted to meet with you.

In the Risen Christ,
Fr Andrew Smith.